HOW MACHINES WORK

AIRCRAFT

IAN GRAHAM

W

FRANKLIN WATTS
LONDON • SYDNEY

 An Appleseed Editions book

First published in 2008 by Franklin Watts

Franklin Watts
338 Euston Road, London NW1 3BH

Franklin Watts Australia
Level 17/207 Kent St, Sydney, NSW 2000

© 2008 Appleseed Editions

Appleseed Editions Ltd
Well House, Friars Hill, Guestling, East Sussex TN35 4ET

Created by Q2AMedia
Series Editor: Honor Head
Book Editor: Harriet McGregor
Senior Art Director: Ashita Murgai
Designers: Harleen Mehta, Mansi Mittal, Shilpi Sarkar
Picture Researchers: Amit Tigga, Poloumi Ghosh

ISBN 978 0 7496 8077 0

Dewey classification: 629.133

All words in **bold** can be found in 'Glossary' on pages 30–31.

Website information is correct at time of going to press. However, the publishers cannot
accept liability for any information or links found on third-party websites.

A CIP catalogue for this book is available from the British Library.

Picture credits
t=top b=bottom c=centre l=left r=right m=middle
Cover Images: Main Image: © 2207 theflightcollection.com

Theflightcollection.com: 4, Colin & Linda McKie/ Shutterstock: 5t, Tim Jenner/ Shutterstock: 5b, Airbus 2006 -Abac effect
– HCSM: 6t, Rolls-royce: 6b, Airbus S.A.S 2005: 8, prism_68/ Shutterstock: 9t, Frank Ungrad/ Shutterstock: 9b,
Mlenny/ Istockphoto: 10b, Piotr Michal (PioM) Jaworski: 11, George Hall/ Corbis: 12, Berkaviation/ Dreamstime: 13t,
Hashim Pudiyapura/ Shutterstock: 13b, Adam Romanowicz/ Shutterstock: 16, Sierrarat/ Istockphoto: 17t,
bbossom/ Istockphoto: 17b, Aircraft Spruce Marketing/ 18t, Adventure_Photo/ Istockphoto: 18b, Science Photo Library: 19b,
Horizon International Images Limited/ Alamy: 20, Maxian/ Istockphoto: 21t, The Boeing Company: 22,
WoodyStock/ Alamy: 23, Paul Souders/ Corbis: 24, U.S. Air Force: 25t, 25b, The Boeing Company: 26,
U.S. Air Force: 28, 29b, Charles F McCarthy/ Shutterstock: 29t

Q2AMedia Art Bank: 7, 10m, 14, 15, 19t, 21, 27

Printed in Hong Kong

Franklin Watts is a division of Hachette Children's Books

CONTENTS

AIRCRAFT

Aircraft are amazing machines. The biggest aircraft can carry hundreds of passengers half way round the world. The fastest can fly faster than a bullet.

SPEED AND HEIGHT

A modern airliner zooms along more than 10,000 metres above the ground. Passengers sit comfortably and hardly notice that it is moving at all. It is an almost perfect combination of power, shape and advanced technology.

The Boeing 787 Dreamliner is Boeing's latest and most advanced airliner

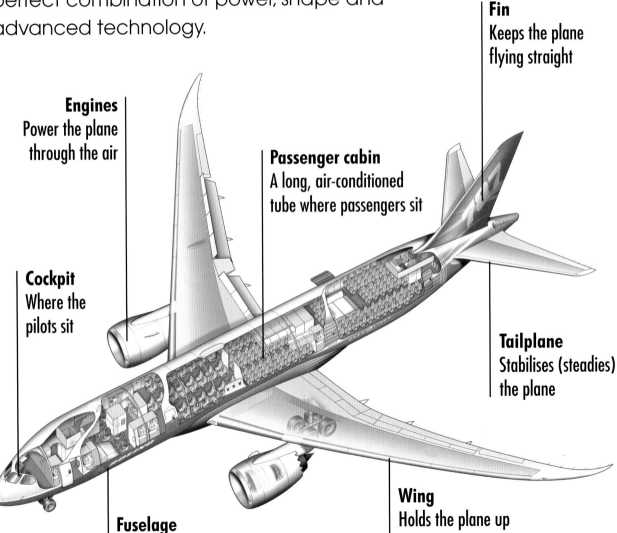

Fin
Keeps the plane flying straight

Engines
Power the plane through the air

Passenger cabin
A long, air-conditioned tube where passengers sit

Cockpit
Where the pilots sit

Tailplane
Stabilises (steadies) the plane

Fuselage
The plane's body

Wing
Holds the plane up in the air

AIRCRAFT TYPES

There are lots of different types of aircraft. Airliners carry lots of passengers, **cargo planes** carry goods, light and ultralight planes are used for fun and transport, and business jets are used as air taxis. There are also many kinds of helicopters and military aircraft. All of these aircraft have engines, but there are also gliders that sail on air currents without any engine power at all.

◀ The smallest ultralight aircraft are just big enough for one person

AIRBUS A380

Specification

Length:	73.0 m (239.5 ft)
Wingspan:	79.8 m (261.8 ft)
Height:	24.1 m (79.1 ft)
Capacity:	850 passengers
Number of engines:	4

▼ The Airbus A380 is the world's biggest airliner. It can carry up to 850 passengers

AIRCRAFT ENGINES

An aircraft engine's job is to provide the power to push the aircraft along the runway and up through the air. Different sized aeroplanes have different types of engine.

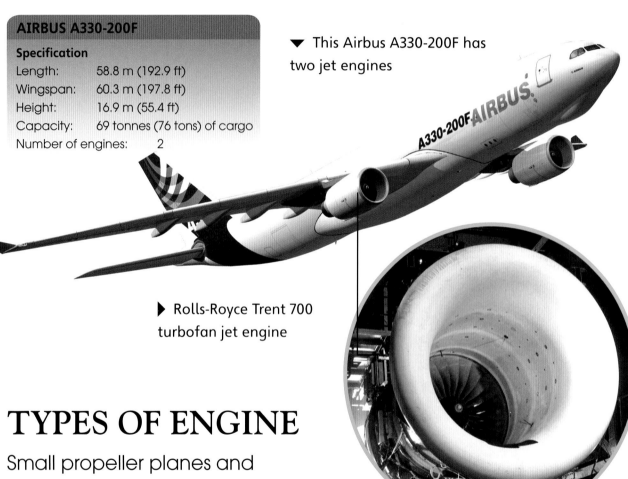

AIRBUS A330-200F

Specification

Length:	58.8 m (192.9 ft)
Wingspan:	60.3 m (197.8 ft)
Height:	16.9 m (55.4 ft)
Capacity:	69 tonnes (76 tons) of cargo
Number of engines:	2

▼ This Airbus A330-200F has two jet engines

▶ Rolls-Royce Trent 700 turbofan jet engine

TYPES OF ENGINE

Small propeller planes and helicopters have piston engines. They work like car engines, but instead of turning wheels, they turn propellers or **rotor blades**. Bigger propeller planes and helicopters have **jet engines**. A jet engine that turns a propeller is called a turboprop. A jet engine that powers a helicopter is called a turboshaft. Faster planes are powered by jet engines called **turbofans**.

HOW DOES A JET ENGINE WORK?

TURBOFAN

▼ The power of a turbofan engine is provided by heating air to make it expand rapidly and produce a high-speed jet

7. Turbine
The hot air spins a **turbine**, which powers the fan and compressor

5. Fuel injector
Sprays fuel into the air

1. Primary air stream
Air is sucked into the centre of the engine by the fan

3. Outer nozzle
Directs the secondary air stream backwards

Fan

8. Hot gases
Thrust the plane forwards

2. Secondary air stream
Air blown around the centre of the engine by the fan

4. Compressor
Some of the air enters a **compressor**, which squashes it

6. Combustion chamber
Fuel burns and heats the air

DID YOU KNOW?
Each of an airliner's jet engines is more powerful than 1,000 family cars!

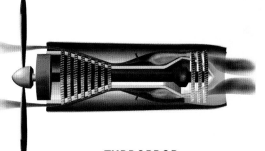

TURBOPROP
A jet engine that drives a propeller

TURBOSHAFT
A jet engine that drives a shaft

7

WHERE'S THE ENGINE?

The engines of most airliners hang below the **wings**. This makes them easy for engineers to get to when they have to be checked or repaired. This works well for **airliners**, but not for fighter planes. Engines under a fighter's wings could be easily damaged by enemy guns and missiles. The engines on fighter planes are hidden inside the aircraft's body.

Engine nacelle
The case that holds the engine

Some jet airliners have two or four engines hanging underneath their wings

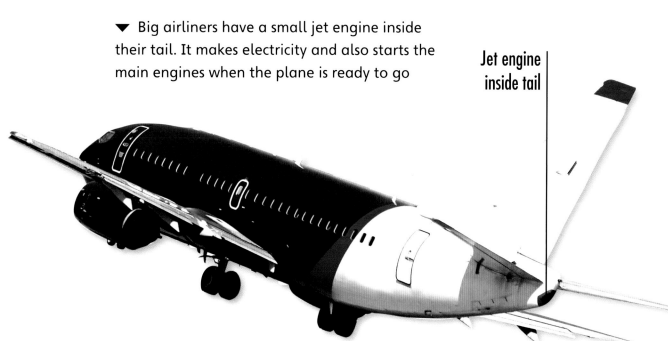

▼ Big airliners have a small jet engine inside their tail. It makes electricity and also starts the main engines when the plane is ready to go

Jet engine inside tail

MORE POWER?

Fighter planes can produce a quick burst of extra power and speed if they need it. They might need more power to take off from a short runway, or more speed to escape an enemy plane. They get the boost of power by turning on their afterburner. The afterburner sprays extra **fuel** into the hot jet coming from the engine. The fuel burns instantly and gives the plane an extra push.

DID YOU KNOW?
A jet engine with its afterburner turned on is said to be working wet!

Afterburner
Inside the engine exhaust nozzle

▲ Turning on an afterburner sends a jet of flame flying from a fighter's engine

TAKING OFF

Planes can take off and fly because of the shape of their wings. Surprisingly, a plane's wings change size and shape during a flight!

WHAT WINGS DO

When a plane's wings move through air, their shape makes the air travel further over the top than underneath. This simple difference produces a force called **lift** that pushes the wings upwards. Tilting the wings up at the front produces even more lift. The special shape of a wing is called an **aerofoil**. The faster an aerofoil moves, the more lift it produces.

A plane takes off when its wings lift upwards more than its weight pulls downwards

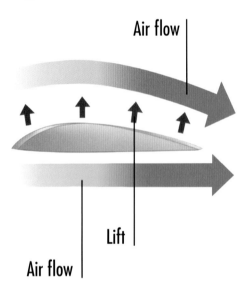

Air flow

Lift

Air flow

Wing
Made of plastic

◀ A sailplane's wings are long and thin for gliding on air currents

DID YOU KNOW?
A glider climbs higher by hitching a ride on rising air currents.

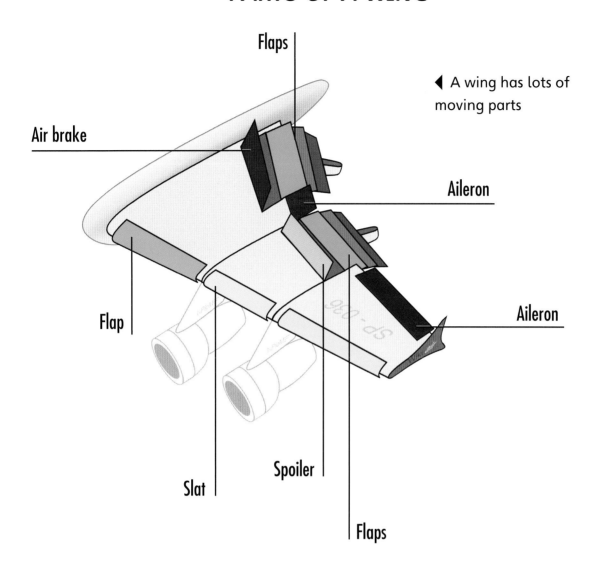

Flaps

◀ A wing has lots of moving parts

Air brake

Aileron

Aileron

Flap

Slat

Spoiler

Flaps

THE PARTS OF A WING

An airliner's wings have moving parts that change their size and shape.

- Flaps and slats slide out from the front and back of wings. They make wings bigger and more curved so that they produce more lift. They are used when a plane is flying slowly for take-off and landing.
- Air brakes swing up on top of a wing to slow a plane down.
- Spoilers 'spoil' (change) the shape of a wing and reduce the amount of lift it produces.
- Strips called **ailerons** tilt up or down to steer a plane.

WING STORAGE

A plane's wings have a lot of room inside. Most of the space is full of fuel, because the wings are a plane's fuel tanks. There are also spaces inside the wings and body where the wheels fold away after take-off. When the wheels are safely tucked inside, doors close over them to give the plane a smooth shape.

DID YOU KNOW?
A Jumbo Jet's wings hold enough fuel to fill the tanks of more than 3,000 cars!

Landing gear
Raised just after take-off to make the plane more streamlined

An airliner's wheels fold up inside its wings and body just after take-off

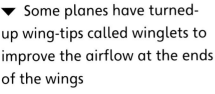

▼ Some planes have turned-up wing-tips called winglets to improve the airflow at the ends of the wings

Flaps
Lowered for landing

Winglet

SPINNING WINGS

The spinning blades on top of a helicopter are long thin wings. When they whirl around, they lift the helicopter into the air. Helicopters can hover (stay in one place in the air). This is because their spinning blades produce lift even when the helicopter itself is not moving. Most planes with wings cannot hover because their wings only produce lift when the plane is moving.

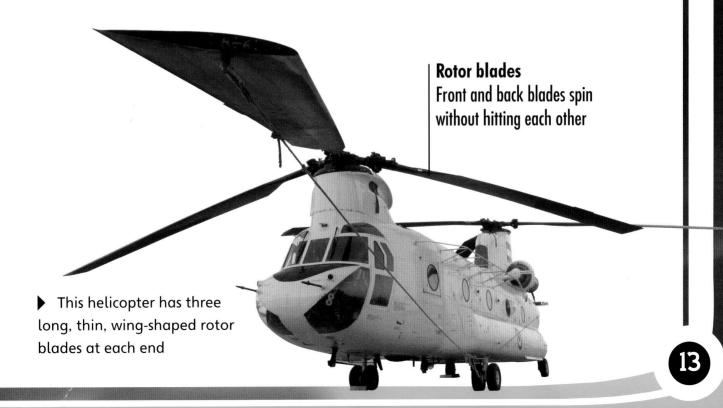

Rotor blades
Front and back blades spin without hitting each other

▶ This helicopter has three long, thin, wing-shaped rotor blades at each end

STEERING AIRCRAFT

A pilot steers a plane by moving parts of its wings and tail. This changes the way air flows around the plane and turns it or tips it to point in a new direction.

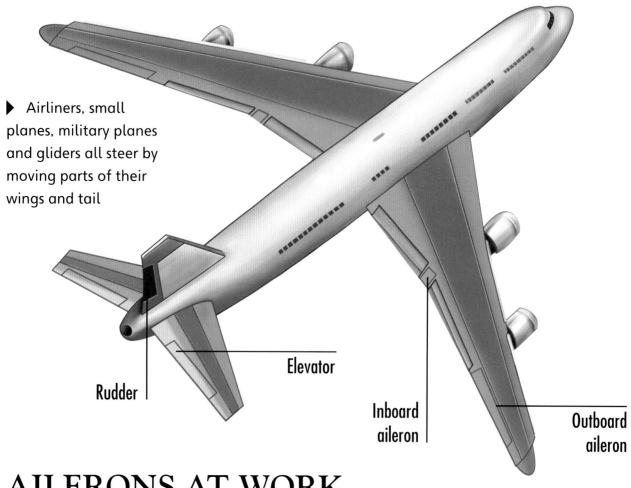

▶ Airliners, small planes, military planes and gliders all steer by moving parts of their wings and tail

Rudder

Elevator

Inboard aileron

Outboard aileron

AILERONS AT WORK

Parts of a plane's wings and tail move to steer the plane. These parts are called control surfaces. The control surfaces in the wings are called ailerons. When the aileron in one wing tilts up, air pushes the wing down. At the same time, the aileron in the other wing tilts down and pushes that wing up. One wing rises, the other wing falls and the plane **rolls** (turns).

PITCH, ROLL AND YAW

A plane can be tilted or turned in three ways.

- It can tip its nose up or down. This is called **pitch**.
- It can raise one wing or the other. This is called roll.
- It can turn its nose to the left or right. This is called **yaw**.

Pitch is controlled by the **elevators**. Roll is controlled by the ailerons. Yaw is controlled by the **rudder**.

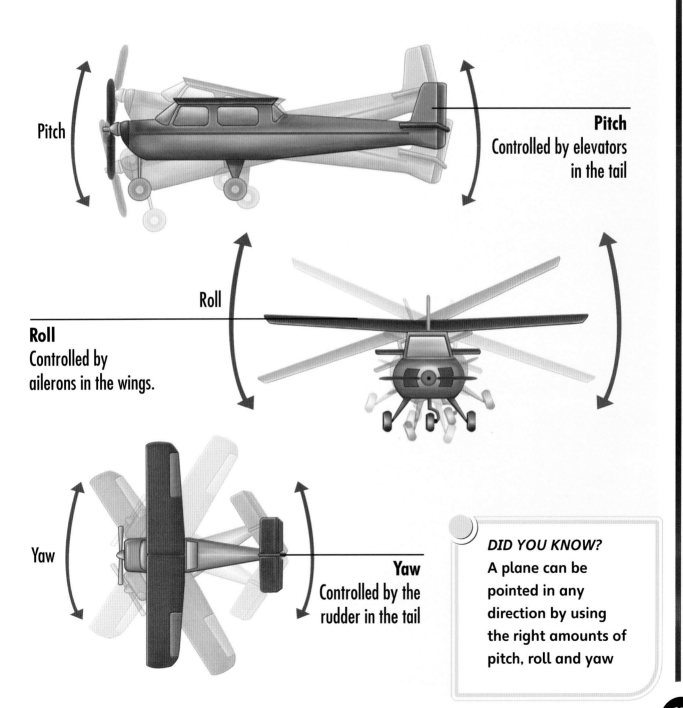

Pitch

Pitch
Controlled by elevators
in the tail

Roll

Roll
Controlled by
ailerons in the wings.

Yaw

Yaw
Controlled by the
rudder in the tail

DID YOU KNOW?
A plane can be
pointed in any
direction by using
the right amounts of
pitch, roll and yaw

HOVER-PLANE

The Harrier jump jet is a very unusual plane. It can take off straight up in the air and hover like a helicopter. It can fly like this because it can point the jet of air from its engine straight downwards. When it is hovering, the pilot tilts and turns the plane by using small jets of air from its nose, tail or wing-tips. When it flies faster, it steers in the same way as other planes.

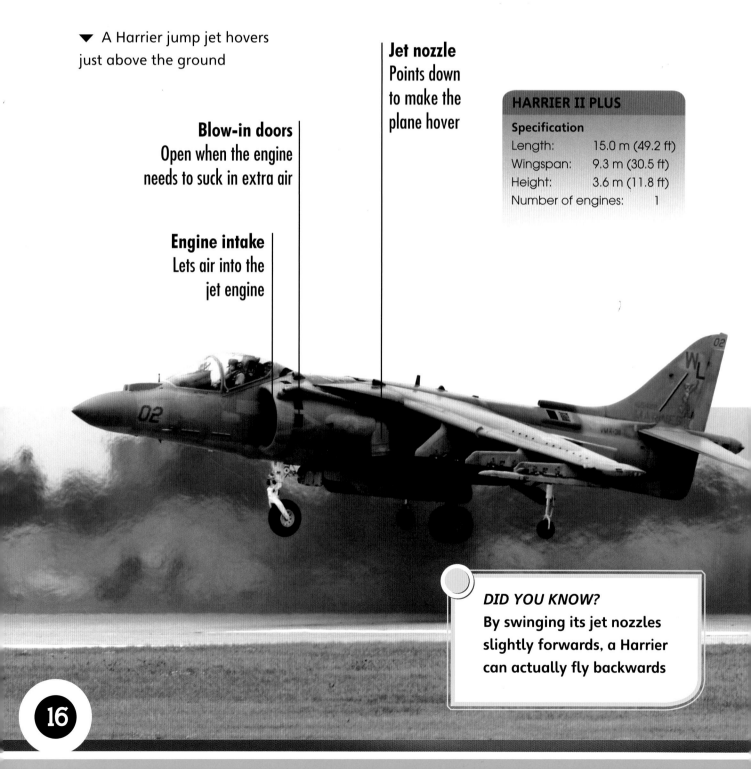

▼ A Harrier jump jet hovers just above the ground

Jet nozzle
Points down to make the plane hover

Blow-in doors
Open when the engine needs to suck in extra air

Engine intake
Lets air into the jet engine

HARRIER II PLUS	
Specification	
Length:	15.0 m (49.2 ft)
Wingspan:	9.3 m (30.5 ft)
Height:	3.6 m (11.8 ft)
Number of engines:	1

DID YOU KNOW?
By swinging its jet nozzles slightly forwards, a Harrier can actually fly backwards

STEERING A HELICOPTER

Helicopters are steered in a different way from aeroplanes. When they are flying straight, a helicopter's blades push air downwards. To turn, helicopters tilt the big rotor on top. Some of the air is now pushed to one side. This blows the helicopter in the opposite direction. The tiny rotor in a helicopter's tail turns the tail. This points the helicopter in the right direction.

Main rotor

▶ Tilting a helicopter's main rotor makes the helicopter turn

Tail rotor

BELL 407

Specification

Length:	12.7 m (41.7 ft)
Rotor diameter:	10.7 m (35.1 ft)
Height:	3.6 m (11.8 ft)
Capacity:	6 passengers
Number of engines:	1

▼ A helicopter's tail rotor stops a helicopter from spinning in the opposite direction to the main rotor

DID YOU KNOW?
The world's fastest helicopter is a Westland Lynx, which set a record of 400 km/h in 1986

17

FINDING THE WAY

Finding the way from place to place is called navigation. Aircraft have navigation equipment to help the pilot fly in the right direction.

STAYING ON COURSE

The simplest way to navigate is to use a **compass**. A compass needle always points north. Aircraft have compasses but they usually have other ways to navigate too. Radio transmitters on the ground send out radio signals. Aircraft receive these signals, so pilots can use them to fly from transmitter to transmitter.

▶ An ordinary compass needle swings about too much in a moving plane. Planes need a steadier compass called a heading indicator or directional gyro, like this one

The reading at the aircraft's nose shows the direction the plane is flying in

◀ Radio transmitters are also called beacons. Beacons like this send out radio signals to guide aircraft

DID YOU KNOW?
Navigation satellites were first used to help submarines work out where they were in the ocean

SATELLITE NAVIGATION

Many aircraft also use satellite navigation or 'satnav' systems. These systems use radio signals from spacecraft to work out where the aircraft is and to make sure it stays on course.

▼ The radio signals from four satellites tell an aircraft where it is

Satellite sends out very accurate time signals

GPS receiver in plane uses satellite signals to work out where it is

SPACE STEERING

Satellites in space travel around the Earth. Some of these are used for satellite navigation, or satnav. These satellites belong to the Global Positioning System (GPS). A radio receiver in an aircraft picks up radio signals from some of the satellites. It uses the signals to work out exactly how far away it is from each satellite, and so pinpoints its position.

A navigation satellite carries an amazingly accurate clock. The clock will only gain or lose one second in 300,000 years!

AIR TRAFFIC CONTROL

Pilots cannot fly wherever they want to. They follow directions from air traffic controllers on the ground. This is especially important in the busy skies around airports. The controllers watch the movements of aircraft on **radar** screens and talk to the pilots by radio. The planes are guided along invisible paths in the sky that keep them a safe distance apart.

▼ An air traffic controller watches aircraft movements on a radar screen

Screens
Show maps of the ground with the airways drawn on top

◀ This radar antenna at London's Heathrow Airport spins around, spotting planes moving around the airport

Radar spots planes when they are too far away to see.

Radar signals
Reflected back to the aerial by the plane

RADAR

Radar uses radio waves to find aircraft. The radar antenna at air traffic control sends out radio waves in all directions. If they hit an aircraft, they bounce off it. Some of the waves bounce straight back to where they came from. These reflections, or echoes, make a bright spot on a radar screen that shows where the aircraft is.

Radar tower

IN THE COCKPIT

An aircraft's cockpit is its control centre. It is the place where the pilot, or pilots, sit and fly the aircraft. The cockpit is in an aircraft's nose.

CONTROLS

The cockpit has all the controls and instruments needed to fly an aircraft. In modern cockpits, most of the instruments have been replaced by flat panel display screens. The screens show the crew all they need, including the aircraft's speed, height, direction and engine performance.

▼ Screens in an airliner cockpit are linked to the plane's computers

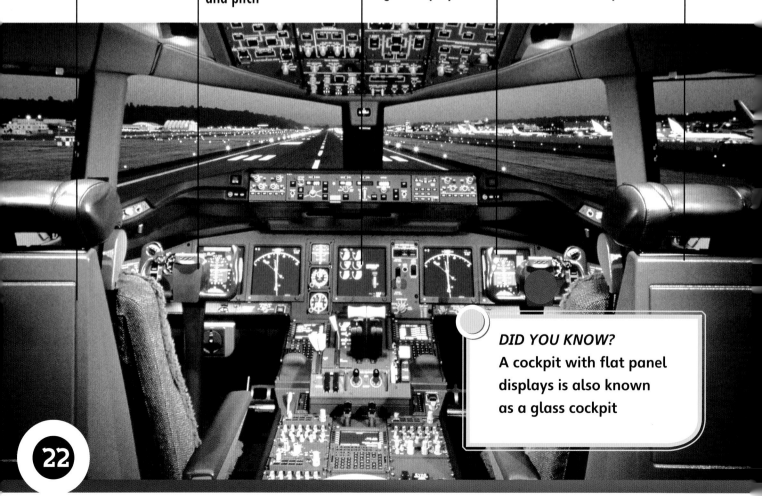

Captain's seat

Control column
Controls roll and pitch

Primary flight display

Engine display

Co-pilot's seat

DID YOU KNOW?
A cockpit with flat panel displays is also known as a glass cockpit

Navigation display

Sidestick controller

IN THE PILOT'S SEAT

Most planes have a control column between the pilot's knees and rudder pedals on the floor. These are the main controls that are used to fly the plane. Moving the control column makes the plane go higher or lower, or bank (roll). Pushing the rudder pedals turns a plane's nose to the left or right. Some airliners do not have control columns. Instead, they are steered by a small hand control, called a sidestick controller, at each side of the cockpit.

The giant Airbus A380 airliner is steered by a tiny control stick no bigger than the pilot's hand

Thrust levers
Control the power levels of the jet engines

FLYING A HELICOPTER

A helicopter has three main controls.The cyclic stick is for steering. The collective lever is moved by the pilot's left hand. Pulling it up tilts the spinning blades and produces more lift for take-off. The rudder pedals control the small tail rotor to keep the helicopter pointing in the right direction.

A helicopter pilot's left hand controls the aircraft's height. The right hand and feet control steering and direction

Cyclic stick
Controls steering

Collective lever
Controls height

Radio microphone
Allows pilot to talk to base

FIGHTER COCKPIT

The **cockpit** of a fighter plane is tiny and cramped. A fighter pilot often doesn't have time to look down at the instruments, so important information appears on a glass screen in front of them. The screen lets the pilot see the information and at the same time look at the sky ahead.

Head-up display panel

▶ A fighter pilot looks out through the greenish glass of the cockpit head-up display

ROCKET SEAT

If a fighter pilot has to get out of a plane in an emergency, a rocket under the seat is fired. It sends the **ejection seat** and pilot flying out of the cockpit. The pilot floats to the ground using a parachute.

Cockpit canopy
Blown clear before the pilot ejects

Pilot strapped into ejection seat

▶ A pilot from the US Air Force Thunderbirds display team ejects from his cockpit during an air display

AIRCRAFT DESIGN

Every aircraft is designed for a purpose. Airliners have a big body for carrying lots of passengers. Fighter planes are small, fast and carry weapons.

BUILDING PLANES

Materials for planes have to be strong and light. Mostly a metal called **aluminium** is used. First, an aluminium frame is made. Then, thin sheets of aluminium are laid on top to make the plane's smooth shape. Some aircraft are made from lighter, stronger metals such as titanium. To save even more weight, some parts are made of plastic.

A line of Boeing 747-400 Jumbo Jets are built inside a giant aircraft construction hall

RIB AND SPAR

The frame inside a plane's wings is like a skeleton. It is made of parts called **ribs** and **spars**. Ribs go from the front of the wing to the back. They give the wing its curved aerofoil shape. Spars are the parts that go from the plane's body to the wing-tip. Spars are incredibly strong because they have to hold up the whole weight of the aircraft.

▼ The moving parts of a wing are fixed to the ribs and spars.

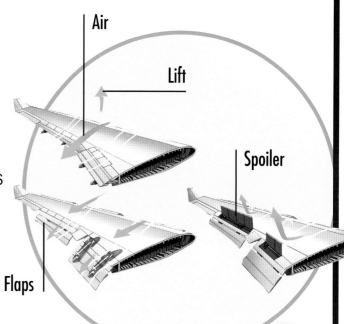

Air

Lift

Spoiler

Flaps

▼ Ribs and spars give wings their shape and strength

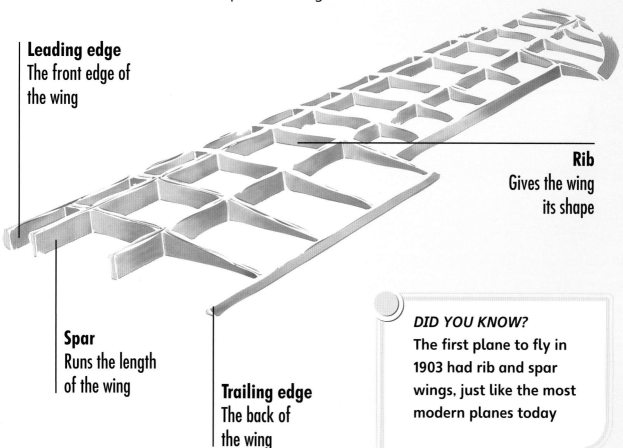

Leading edge
The front edge of the wing

Rib
Gives the wing its shape

Spar
Runs the length of the wing

Trailing edge
The back of the wing

DID YOU KNOW?
The first plane to fly in 1903 had rib and spar wings, just like the most modern planes today

Tail fins
Angled to make
the plane more
stealthy

Intakes
Bring lots of air
in for the plane's
two powerful
jet engines

SUPERSONIC

Most aircraft fly slower than the
speed of sound. Sound travels
through the air at about 1,200
km/h . The fastest military planes
can fly faster than sound. They are
supersonic. Incredibly, some fighters
can fly at more than three times
the speed of sound. They have
to be exactly the right shape to
slice through the air at such a high
speed. They need a sharp nose, a
slim body and thin wings.

The F-22A Raptor is
a fighter designed
to fly at twice the
speed of sound

DID YOU KNOW?
The speed of sound is
also known as mach 1.
The fastest aircraft can
reach mach 3, three times
the speed of sound

STEALTH PLANES

Aircraft far away in the sky are spotted by radar. The aircraft show up as bright spots moving across a radar screen. Some warplanes are specially designed so that they do not make bright dots on radar screens. Planes like this are called **stealth planes**. They are able to hide from enemy radar. It is their shape and the materials they are made from that allow them to do this. Stealth lets warplanes close in on their target without being spotted.

▼ The B-2 can travel 9,600 km before it needs to refuel

NORTHROP B-2 SPIRIT

Specification

Length:	20.9 m (68.6 ft)
Wingspan:	52.1 m (170.9 ft)
Height:	5.1 m (16.7 ft)
Capacity:	2 (crew)
Number of engines:	4

Engines
On top to shield them from heat-seeking missiles

Weapons
Carried in two bays inside the plane's body

Wing
Made of strong plastic

Cockpit
With room for a crew of two

The B-2 Spirit bomber is a stealth plane. Its strange shape, with no body or tail, is called a flying wing

29

GLOSSARY

Aerofoil Shape of a wing that produces lift

Aileron Part of a plane's wing that swivels up or down to make the plane roll

Airliner Plane designed to carry paying passengers

Aluminium Lightweight metal used to build aircraft

Cargo Goods carried by an aircraft

Cargo plane Aircraft that carries goods

Cockpit Control centre of a plane, where the pilot sits

Compressor Part of a jet engine that squashes air inside the engine

Combustion Burning

Combustion Chamber Part of a jet engine where the fuel is burned

Compass Instrument for showing directions

Ejection seat Rocket-propelled pilot's seat in a fighter plane

Elevator Part of a plane's tail that swivels up or down to make the plane's nose tip up or down

Fin Part of an aircraft's tail that stands up

Fuel Substance that is burned to produce heat or power

Helicopter Aircraft that has rotor blades and is able to hover in the air

Jet engine Type of engine that works by producing a fast jet of air

Lift Upwards force produced by an aircraft's wings or a helicopter's rotor blades

Navigation Setting a route and steering a plane along it

Pitch One of the three ways an aircraft can tilt or turn. When an aircraft pitches, its nose rises or falls

Radar Method for finding aircraft by bouncing radio waves off them

Rib Part of the frame inside a wing, running from front to back

Roll One way that an aircraft can turn. When an aircraft rolls, one wing rises and the other falls

Rotor blade Long thin wing-shaped part of a helicopter that spins

Rudder Part of an aircraft's tail fin that swivels to turn the aircraft's nose to the right or left

Spar Part of the frame inside a wing, running from the plane's body to the tip of the wing

Supersonic Faster than the speed of sound

Stealth plane Plane that is hard to find by radar because of its shape and the materials it is made from

Thrust Force that pushes a plane through the air

Turbine Part of a jet engine that looks like a propeller with lots of blades

Turbofan Type of jet engine with a large fan at the front to suck in air

Wing Large part of a plane that produces lift when it moves through air

Winglet Small turned-up wing-tip

Yaw One of the three ways an aircraft can tilt or turn. When an aircraft yaws, its nose turns to the left or right

INDEX

Websites

www.boeing.com/companyoffices/aboutus/wonder_of_flight/index.html
Find out how things fly

www.nasa.gov/audience/forkids/home/F_How_Do_Planes_Fly_Slideshow.html
Watch the slide show to find out about lift, thrust and drag

www.boeing.com/companyoffices/aboutus/kids
Pictures to colour, cut-outs and games to play, all about aircraft